No Natural Weather
Introduction to Geoengineering 101
By
WeatherWar101

Contents

Foreword

Once upon a time, all over the world, we saw fluffy white clouds in a blue sky. Today we see white lines and streaks, and many of us, in many countries, live under a layer of white haze. Children no longer know what real clouds look like, as the three basic cloud types are no longer seen. Remember the high-altitude cirrus, feathery and white, made of ice crystals? I have not seen real cirrus clouds for 15 years. What occurs now is what NASA calls "man-made cirrus" or "jet cirrus" – an actual admission of something unnatural and artificial.

Some time ago, the U.S. Air Force released a famous document called "Owning the Weather in 2025." The reality is that someone owns the weather today, having introduced agents of change into our atmosphere on a regular basis. In this series by WeatherWar101 you will learn about how and why these change agents are being used, and better yet, you will learn to SEE that the world is no longer as it used to be. When changes happen slowly and authorities tell us all is well, we continue to place our trust in "normalcy" despite our instincts prodding us that things are different and wrong.

Storms no longer feel like storms. Remember that charged feeling in the air as the sky got darker and you rushed home to close the windows? People's hair would frizz before it rained, and after the rain the air would feel so clean, sunshine dancing off the tops of the beautiful cotton-candy cumulus that drifted in. None of that pre-storm natural electricity occurs today, and no one talks about their hair frizzing. The fact is that our storms are man-made, and they have gotten bigger and stronger. We are being told this is Mother Nature's act of war against us – against our air pollution and the atmospheric warming we are responsible for. Not so. The weather itself has been weaponized without our consent, and most of us are none the wiser.

"No Natural Weather" is a clearly written simple tutorial about weather modification and much more, designed for newcomers to the concept, but also full of explanations and clarifications that will add to the research of those who are already aware. Start at the beginning and let this narrative take you on a journey from soup to nuts, A to Z. Share the series with your family and friends! There is no better time than now to educate yourself to what is and has been going on, and the thoughtful guidance provided by this seasoned researcher is the best company you could have on such an alarming journey. For yes, it is alarming to learn that our planet is being altered in ways that it may never recover from. It is time for us all to voice our collective power, but no one can do so until the actual knowledge has been given and shared. Thank you, WeatherWar101, for your immense contribution!

Sofia Smallstorm

Introduction

As I said in the post comment on my 105th video on geoengineering, few would find my particular Groundhog's Day enjoyable (if at all tolerable). The reality of "No Natural Weather" on this planet anymore has been very clear to me for a long time now, but trying to get this critical and foundational knowledge to the people of this planet – who desperately need it to understand the world they live in – has proven to be much more difficult and challenging than understanding the reality of Global Geoengineering itself.

For several years now I have been teaching to a very small group of individuals the reality of our geoengineered world, but it hasn't been a small group by choice. I won't spend any time on it now, but as you come to understand the size and scope of the global geoengineering program, the length of time this global operation has been in development and in place, and the shockingly long period that it was well known that the catastrophic situation this planet is in now would be the inevitable result of industrialization (as is), it will become very clear why getting this information to the general public has been met with such resistance.

However, there isn't any way to hide this reality anymore for a great many reasons. First of all, the evidence is everywhere. Every day on the news they show it, and every time you walk out of your house you see it. Every single living creature on this planet is living in it, breathing it, eating it, and drinking it, and there just isn't any way to pretend it isn't happening anymore. Every day in the city streets I hear it – more and more people are finding the endless and bizarre manufactured weather patterns we are increasingly subjected to as quite literally "unbelievable." As much effort goes into covering up this long running and obvious reality, people are still clearly seeing it for what it is… even though they have no understanding of how or why it is happening.

More importantly than that, it is every living thinking beings right to understand the state of the planet they live on, how it got into this dire condition, and what we can possibly do about salvaging the future environment on this planet. The story of how this geoengineering behemoth was created and why no one knows about it spans over a hundred years. No one who started the people of this planet off on this disastrous path is alive today to be held responsible and I'm quite sure the geoengineers operating in secret now view it as having no choice, but it wasn't the original perpetrators' right to send this planet and all life on it down the course to destruction the way they did, nor is it the current geoengineers right to keep this massive planetary lie from the seven billion people affected and subjected to it either.

The people of this planet need to be fully aware of the reasons, their unknowing involvement, and the massive repercussions of the state of the global environment. The geoengineers have demonstrated in many disturbing ways that they will not be able to compensate for the continuing damage being done, nor do they have critical interests in mind that are required to address this catastrophe. For there to be a future on this planet, seven billion people are going to need to be informed of reality… which means waking up from a 100-year delusion.

Awakened @piKKKil · 14h
Regardless the causes or effects, it seems to be too complex for the masses to ever maintain a logical grip on the truth. @WeatherWar101

💬 View conversation   ↩ Reply   ⇄ Retweet   ★ Favorite   ••• More

As I said to my friend, Global Geoengineering is not at all too complex for anyone to understand. In fact, I could teach it to children. Bear in mind, most of the concepts and foundations of global geoengineering were developed and started being implemented 50 to 100 years ago. A society that basically lives in cyberspace and technology at this point, is not going to have a problem understanding concepts developed in the late 1800s and early 1900s. If a child can understand how to use a tablet, then that child will have no problem understanding the fundamental concepts of geoengineering.

So, in this first book of the series I will demonstrate that. I realize how over-saturated people are with information (most of it useless), so I'm going to keep this series simple. It's quite possible that I will develop a more targeted series for young people, but I very much mean it when I say a child can understand this.

Therefore, I will be writing this series in the hopes that in addition to the adults I plan on reaching, that grandparents, parents, aunts, uncles and school teachers will use this series to educate the generations who will actually have to deal with the results of 100 years of greed and denial. The sooner they understand what they will have to deal with, the sooner they can start putting their minds to rectifying the mistakes the generations before them wouldn't even face.

History Overview

Perspective is everything. In 2014, people can't begin to imagine what life without computers, smartphones, the internet, and the many interconnected technologies that run our lives would be like. Nowadays almost everything people do requires electric power in some form, but only 100 years ago the light bulb barely existed, and the power grid on which we all rely didn't exist at all.

The first power station built in this country was Edison's Pearl Street Station[1] in New York in 1882. It was a coal-burning plant providing steam to drive six generators that provided DC (Direct Current) electricity to a one-square-mile area of New York City.

As power and distance needs grew rapidly, the limitations of Edison's DC electric plants became evident, and after a long battle with Nikola Tesla and his partner George Westinghouse over which electrical system was best, AC (Alternating Current) was proven to meet the growing needs, and was adopted as the standard we all know today.

Over the decades these power plants increased dramatically in size and output capability, and many more power plants were built across the country. Today the United States power grid consists of roughly 7,000 individual power plants nationwide.[2] Naturally, power plant development and distribution is very similar in all other industrialized countries as well.

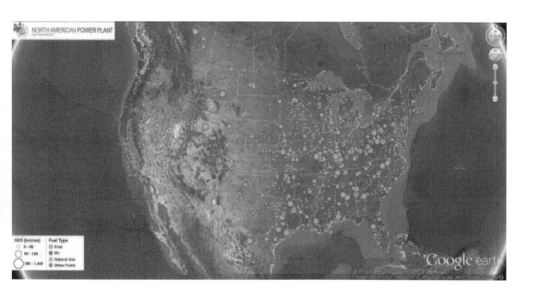

However, one of the problems the very first power plant had in 1882 is a problem power plants worldwide continue to have today. It took an immense amount of coal to produce the steam to drive the generators to produce the electricity needed. In 2014, the primary fuel for power plants worldwide is still the same as it was in 1882. Even with 100 years of efficiency improvements to steam turbines and coal burning power plants, it still requires 714 pounds of coal to run a single 100-watt light bulb for one year. The giant Gibson generating station in southwestern Indiana for instance has five 180-foot-high boilers that burn 25 tons of coal every minute. Just this one station requires three 100-car trainloads of coal a day. Close to eight billion tons of coal are burned annually worldwide.

As ridiculous as it sounds, in 2014 the Global Power Grid still basically runs on the coal-fired steam engine. The fact that all efforts to move from fossil-fuel-burning power generation in the last 100 years have been thwarted at every opportunity is the single pivotal reason for the disaster this planet is in. At the same time, these power plants are the central component of the global geoengineering program – and have been for the last 50 years. As you will come to discover, understanding this relationship is key to understanding the sequence of events that brought us to the precipice we are on today.

Pollution

What is a cloud? In nature, clouds are formed by the process of slow evaporation. Water from the ocean, lakes, puddles, trees, etc., is released into the atmosphere and turned into a cloud.

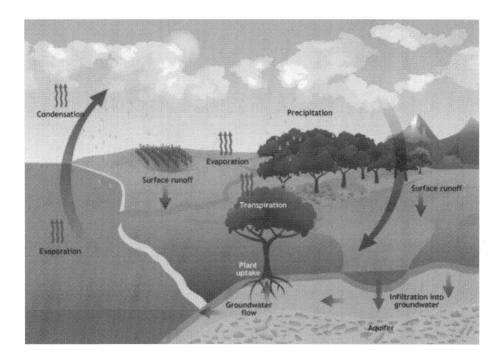

Heat from the Sun hits the water which slowly evaporates and turns into air. That warm air is carried up into the atmosphere and rises. As the warm water vapor rises through the air, a cooling process begins that forms tiny water droplets.

These droplets of water are formed around natural particles in the air like dust and sea salt. All of these droplets expand together and form visible clouds that we see in the sky.

Daniel Rosenfeld, of the Hebrew University of Jerusalem, studied satellite images of smog streaming out of power plants, lead smelters and oil refineries. In a BBC article (March 10th,

2000), he showed that the pollution particles led to the formation of very small droplets that were far too tiny to fall to Earth as rain.[3]

The reason why pollution stops rain and snow is that the particles allow the cloud moisture to condense into much smaller droplets than usual.

It takes about one million normal-sized droplets to collide and coalesce to produce a raindrop large enough to fall to Earth. With the smaller droplets, the chances of collision are much lower and raindrops do not form.

This BBC article on Rosenfeld's conclusions calls this the first direct evidence of how pollution affects rainfall. That statement is quite a long way from being true.

On May 24th, 1953 an article was published in the New York Times titled "How Industry May Change Climate." This article was based on the work of Dr. Gilbert N. Plass of John Hopkins. Sixty years ago, Dr. Plass found that in many ways carbon dioxide (CO_2) and industrial pollution actually stops rain, by preventing, for instance, the strong convection currents (winds) needed for precipitation.

How Industry May Change Climate

The amount of carbon dioxide in the air will double by the year 2080 and raise the temperature an average of at least 4 per cent. The burning of about two billion tons of coal and oil a year keeps the average ground temperature somewhat higher than it would otherwise be. If industrial growth extended over several thousand years instead of over a century only, the oceans would have absorbed most of the excess carbon dioxide. Seas circulate so slowly that they have had little effect in reducing the amount of the gas as man's smoke-making abilities multiplied during a hundred years.

All this and more came out in the course of a paper that Dr. Gilbert N. Plass of Johns Hopkins presented before the American Geophysical Union. He found that man's industries add six billion tons of carbon dioxide to the atmosphere.

Heat Is Retained

Like glass in a greenhouse, carbon dioxide in the air prevents the escape of long-wave radiation (heat) from the ground but allows short wave-length radiation from the sun to pass through. When the amount of the gas increases, the atmospheric blanket holds more heat near the earth's surface. At the same time, the tops of clouds are prevented from losing heat into space as rapidly as before. The drop in temperature variation between the top and bottom layers of clouds prevents the formation of strong convection cur-

rents necessary for the onset of precipitation. This may mean less rainfall and cloud cover, so that still more sunlight can reach the earth's surface. Thus man tends to make his climate warmer and drier; should there be a decrease in carbon dioxide, a cooler and wetter climate would result.

Theory Applied to Glaciers

All this reinforces a theory advanced in 1861 that decreases in carbon dioxide explain the growth and advance of glaciers at various intervals in the earth's history. Dr. Plass finds the theory plausible. If the theory is correct, millions of years of mountain-building preceded each glacial period. During these long periods large quantities of exposed fire-made rock weathered during the uplift of the land, with the result that the amount of free carbon dioxide in the air was greatly reduced. If reduction amounted to only a factor of two, the gas in the atmosphere would have been reduced fivefold. The consequences have been heavier rainfall and a temperature drop of more than seven degrees.

As the weathering process slowed down, mountains were leveled and gas from inside the earth made its way into the atmosphere, the temperature rose, the climate became drier and the glacier receded. In the future, as in the past, important changes in temperature and rainfall will result from variations in the supply of carbon dioxide.

W. K.

The New York Times
Published: May 24, 1953
Copyright © The New York Times

In 1953 Dr. Plass had already made the case that the Earth could not keep up with 100 years of man's smoke-making ability. You can imagine how much that smoke making ability has increased in the 60 years since then. At the time this article was written two billion tons of coal were being burned per year. Now, eight billion tons of coal are burned a year. This shows beyond any doubt that the long-term impact of pollution was already known over half a century ago, and explains how and why the last 60 years of global geoengineering research, development and implementation have unfolded as they have.

See:

NASA: Changing our Weather, One Smokestack at a Time http://ow.ly/yWbc30bYZUE

IPCC Climate Change 2013: U.N. Report Detailed http://ow.ly/epMb30bYZZD

Nexrad Weather Control - NOAA Aerosols Report Justifying Chemtrailing
http://ow.ly/9lje30bZ05w

Chemtrails

In order for the rising warm air to turn from water vapor to liquid, a particle is needed for the water to condense on. This particle is called a Cloud Condensation Nuclei (CCN), or a "cloud seed." These small particles are usually about 0.2 μm (Microns), or 1/100th the size of a cloud droplet.[4]

There are many different types of particles in the air that can act as CCN. The numbers and types of CCN affect the lifetimes and properties of clouds. Dust, ash from fires and sea salt are the most common natural CCN, but as we have already seen, particles from fossil fuel and industrial pollution can dominate and prevent natural cloud formation. Some particle types make better CCN than others. Salts are particularly good for the formation of droplets. In order to have any clouds form at all in conditions of heavy pollution, many more usable CCN have to be present in the air.

US Patent #5003186: Stratospheric Welsbach Seeding For Reduction Of Global Warming (PDF)

This April 23, 1990 patent describes the main method of putting tiny particles in the air to reduce the effects of Greenhouse gases (CO_2), which is the same process as introducing CCN particles.[5] "One proposed solution to the problem of global warming involves the seeding of the atmosphere with metallic particles. One technique proposed to seed the metallic particles was to add the tiny particles to the fuel of jet airliners, so that the particles would be emitted from the jet-engine exhaust while the airliner was at its cruising altitude."

"Such materials can include the class of materials known as Welsbach materials. The oxides of metal, e.g., aluminum oxide, are also suitable for the purpose."

This is the principle behind chemtrails, and it is why all over the world, every day, many people see and document skies that look like this:

These oxides of metal (aluminum oxide, barium oxide, etc.) make very good Cloud Condensation Nuclei, and under chemical reaction can also be turned into salts. In this way usable CCN are added to the atmosphere in huge amounts on a daily and visible basis.

See:
Geoengineering: Analytika Chemtrail Lab Results http://ow.ly/KHUX30bZ09C
Geoengineering: Chemtrailing Sochi Olympics http://ow.ly/uYqR30bZ0h7
Nano Skies Movie: Chemtrails Revealed http://ow.ly/yjGc30bZ0kC

Water Vapor Generation

Most of the Earth is covered with oceans, and in the natural evaporation cycle, most of the water vapor in the atmosphere would come from evaporation from the oceans. However, for reasons that will be covered later in this series, the natural evaporation cycle on this planet is severely damaged, and has been for a very long time. The geoengineers have known about this problem for an equally long period of time, and have been building a system to compensate for the lack of natural evaporation for over half a century.

In the natural cycle, Water Vapor is formed by slow evaporation. In geoengineering, Water Vapor comes from generating steam. Instead of the Sun slowly heating the Earth's oceans and lakes and water vapor slowly rising, Water Vapor Generation is more like boiling water in a tea kettle. When the water reaches boiling, the steam (Water Vapor) streams out of the tea kettle and into the air.

To shoot Water Vapor into the air for geoengineering, you would need very big tea kettles and a great many of them. You would need them all over the world to feed the Water Vapor Stream (Atmospheric River), and you would need to control them in sequence. Can you guess how this is done? As I said earlier, the biggest cause of global pollution is also the biggest component in global geoengineering. Our planet is covered in coal-burning furnaces that produce steam for power generation, and these furnaces are also the source of Water Vapor Generation for Global Geoengineering.

Power Station Water Vapor Generation is very easy to identify once you understand a few simple points. When looking at a satellite image of the Earth, Water Vapor in the natural process would be observed slowly developing over the oceans and large bodies of water, and then moving over the land masses.

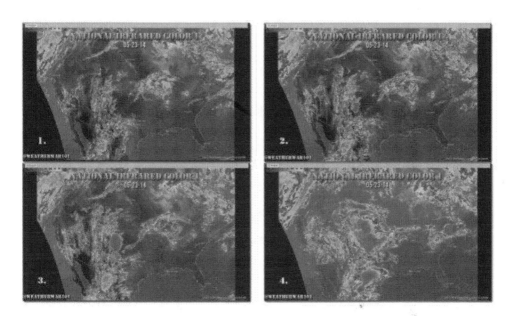

However, that is not what we see at all on a daily basis. What we see instead is many individual circular bursts of Water Vapor suddenly appearing, not over the oceans and large bodies of water, but above the mainland continents and island land masses. This is evidence of the Power Plant Tea Kettles sending Super-Heated Water Vapor in the air. The sequence is visible over the entire planet, and it cycles repeatedly every day. It is the most obvious and telling sign of the scope of the Global Geoengineering Program.

I have gone back (60+ years) to the earliest weather satellite images I can find, and have never found an image that did not have this geoengineering signature. This proves one very important thing: For much longer than satellite imaging has been available, the Water Vapor/Evaporation problem was not only well known, but systems to compensate for it (while continuing to cause the problem to begin with) were already being developed. For me personally, this was one of the most difficult realities of Global Geoengineering to accept. Such a very long time trying to compensate without facing the actual cause, and such a very long time keeping the world's population in the dark.

See:

Proof: Worldwide Massive Flooding is All Manmade http://ow.ly/7Tby30bZ0pt

Colorado Flooding is All Manmade http://ow.ly/3P2030bZ0BB

Nexrad Frequency Control

We have shown how these huge cloud systems are created, but how are they spun up into the superstorms we see twice a week? Controlling these systems requires an enormous amount of frequency acting on them all the time to speed them up, change their directions, and combine them.

Radar (RAdio Detection And Ranging) is a system that uses radio waves to determine the range, altitude, direction or speed of objects. The radar dish or antenna transmits pulses of radio waves or microwaves that bounce off any object in their path. The object returns a tiny part of the wave's energy to a dish or antenna. Radar signals are reflected especially well by materials of considerable electrical conductivity: most metals, seawater and by wetlands.[6]

The "Frequency" of these microwave pulses is the number of times the wave cycles in one second. This measurement is expressed in Hertz (Hz): 1Hz = 1 cycle per second. 7.8Hz is the resonance frequency of Earth and Life, and is known as the Schumann Resonance. The significance of all of this will be covered in much greater detail later in the series.[7]

Those who have heard anything at all about geoengineering (before this book) have heard of the HAARP facility in Alaska. The High Frequency Active Auroral Research Program directs a focused and steerable 3.5 billion watt (3.5 GW – latest stated max) signal (pulsed or continuous) in the 2.8–10 MHz band into the ionosphere. HAARP is a reversal of a radio telescope. It is an antenna that sends out signals instead of receiving, and has been one of the test facilities for super-powerful radio-wave beaming technology for the last couple of decades.

Although many of the methods used today were clearly developed at this facility and others like it around the world, it is not at all responsible for daily global geoengineering. The movement and people claiming that HAARP is primarily responsible for all global weather events are being deliberately misled away from the actual systems responsible for this frequency control, and are ill-informed of the actually reality.[8]

Much more advanced and localized Next Generation Radar (NEXRAD) facilities and towers have been developed in the last two decades. The ability of NEXRAD to perform the same functions as HAARP is easy to observe. In fact, the HAARP facility is of such little use to the Air Force and Geoengineering research at this point that it is scheduled to be dismantled this summer (2014).[9]

Frequency has little effect on pure water vapor. In order to create a cloud that can be controlled, there must be material in and throughout the cloud that frequency can act on. This brings us back to chemtrails. The nano-sized metal and heavy-metal particles (aluminum, barium, etc.) produced from the process described in the Welsbach patent are distributed throughout the atmosphere from jet engines. These metal oxides act as CCN (Cloud Condensation Nuclei) to form droplets of water which combine into clouds. These clouds, now full of metal nano particles, can be acted upon by frequency.

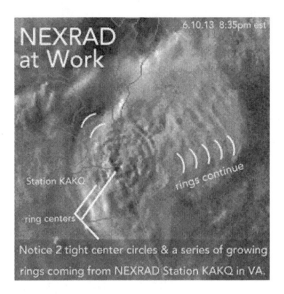

The global frequency net needed to control these Heavy-Metal Nano-Cloud systems has been in development for a very long time, just like the Global Water Vapor Generation System. In 1988 the Nexrad WSR-88D (Next Generation Weather Surveillance Radar 1988 Doppler) was rolled out, and similar Doppler Radar systems cover the rest of the planet, although they are not called

Nexrad. These systems are evenly spaced across the country and across the land masses of the world. These systems have been upgraded and enhanced repeatedly in the last 20 years (e.g., with Dual Polarization), and all evidence indicates that the final Phased Array upgrades are completed as well.[10]

These powerful and plentiful local radar systems have the functionalities of the HAARP facility in Alaska and much, much more. They have the ability to ionize plasma, create huge spinning vortexes, frequency activate Artificial Ice Nucleation, create rolling Nexrad Heterodyne Waves (Gravity Waves), and various other functions (all of which will be detailed later in the series). It is this Global Frequency Grid acting on the Heavy-Metal Nano-Cloud systems that creates the bizarre and wholly unnatural storm systems that we are seeing all across the planet in 2014. There is no natural weather anymore, and there hasn't been in a very long time.

See:

Nexrad Weather Control: Tornado Creation 301 http://ow.ly/Z4dT30bZ11Z

Geoengineering: Polar Vortex - Ice Nucleation 101 http://ow.ly/VOPE30bZ0Li

Geoengineering: Polar Vortex - Part Deux http://ow.ly/Elhk30bZ15O

How Nexrad HAARP Works: Turning Natural Storms into Biblical Floods
http://ow.ly/7cvl30bZ1aO

Other Control Factors and Mechanisms

I have outlined the major components in Global Geoengineering here, but these are certainly not all of the components. For instance, if you take a look at the wind map on any given day, you will see a whole new level of strangeness. Massive swirling in-and-out vortexes spinning in opposite directions, giant flat wind barrier lines, and all kinds of other wholly unnatural-looking anomalies are abundant.

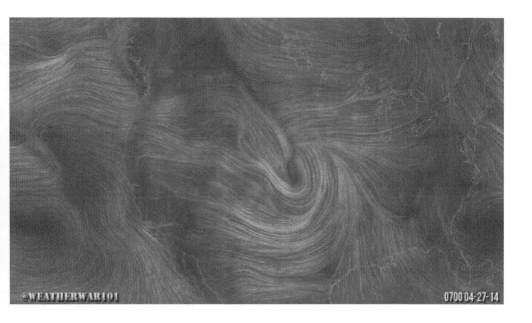

This is the means by which the artificial jet stream is manipulated. The WW101Team is in the process of isolating the exact methodology, but it is clear (and all evidence indicates) that this is accomplished by a network of various types of Orgone Accumulators, largely placed in and around water sources.

Orgone is a Universal Energy first detected by Wilhelm Reich in the 1930s. Although this is a very complex topic, Reich demonstrated the ability to create and dissipate rain by attracting and directing this energy. His research has been developed by numerous scientists over the past 60 years, and there is a large community of people who study Orgone and Orgonite effects on the weather. It is clear this is a major component in creating these vortexes, high-speed winds and sudden cloud formations.[11]

There are also numerous other towers, platforms, sea vessels, etc., involved in the enormous Geoengineering System. These additional aspects will be covered in detail later in this series.

Conclusion

I have deliberately kept this book very short and simple for a couple of reasons. To the newcomer, Global Geoengineering is a daunting and formidable topic. It is a huge transition from thinking the weather is in the hands of Mother Nature to understanding just how much that is not the case, and that realization is enough to digest all by itself. As much as is possible, I don't want to overwhelm anyone with this reality.

Awakened @piKKKil · 14h
Regardless the causes or effects, it seems to be too complex for the masses to ever maintain a logical grip on the truth. @WeatherWar101

💬 View conversation   ↩ Reply   ⟲ Retweet   ★ Favorite   ••• More

Second, hopefully I've demonstrated that Geoengineering is not at all too complex for people to understand. I start and end with this Tweet from my friend as a reminder to myself of what I intended to accomplish, and as a reminder to you, the reader, of the main point you should take away from this book. You can understand this, as can every member of your family… And it's extremely important that you see to it every member of your family *does* understand it.

Lastly I named this first in the series "101" for obvious reasons. There is much more to get into, and I've already started work on "201." My intention for this series is to build incrementally and at a comfortable pace, so this information isn't any more overwhelming than it has to be. The topic is difficult enough without being bombarded with too much information all at once. For those who are anxious to continue their education however, the following playlist of 33 essential videos will get you well on your way.

Introduction to Geoengineering 101
http://ow.ly/AoJA30bZ1hM

However, past the mechanics of Global Geoengineering, there is obviously a very serious societal reality to understand, that has put us all in the position we are in. For 100 years, the people in control of this society and the people who have kept this planet enslaved to fossil fuels as the only source of energy have doomed us to the destroyed and diseased ecosystem we are all living in. Worst of all, they are still lying to us about it, as they have been for the last 100 years.

The physical and scientific realities I have outlined here all exist and are all verifiable, as are all of the systems I have outlined. The fact of the matter is if they were not geoengineering the planet exactly as I have detailed, all of the systems are in place to do it. This leaves you, the reader, with only two possible conclusions: Either I have 'coincidentally' and single-handedly devised a way of geoengineering the world's weather that exactly matches all of the systems in place and all of the weather evidence for the last 50 years, or I am describing the system as it exists.

Thus, to put it as simply as can be imagined, the ecosystem of this planet has been destroyed by coal and oil barons in control of this fossil-fuel economy in order to keep 100 years of fossil-fuel profits running into their coffers. It is why in 2014 the global power grid still runs on the steam engine, it is why combustion engines automobiles still belch oil smoke, and it is why Orgone (Zero Point Energy) is used to mask the disaster and engineer the weather instead of being used to replace the dated technology that is killing the planet and everything on it.

Most disturbing of all is that this has been going on for over half a century without the public's knowledge, and that turning it all off and returning a natural cycle of weather isn't even close to a viable option. Since the natural cycle has been all but destroyed, Geoengineering is the only reason it rains at all. As you will come to see as you study this situation, without the constant global generation of Water Vapor, and without some form of CCN to compensate for the totally polluted atmosphere, it wouldn't rain at all. Additionally, most people have noticed that even when we have one day without engineered cloud cover, the temperature rapidly approaches 100 degrees – no matter where you are.

That is a glimpse of what the "natural" state of this planet is… and it's only getting exponentially worse. Without constant geoengineering in place of the destroyed natural cycle, our planet would be looking like the surface of Mars in no time. In fact, some places already do.

Pop Quiz: Which parts of the planet are being geoengineered, and which parts are not?

Although geoengineering is the only reason there is weather at all, the nightmare in place is no solution either. Between nano-poisoning of the entire environment (the air, the water, the land and the food) and the frequency bombardment and destruction of all natural resonant relationships and balance, the cycle of life on this planet is all but destroyed. Not to mention, we are still not addressing the problem that should have been faced 100 years ago. This species and this planet should not be running on burning fossil fuels - anymore.

Much more intelligent and farsighted solutions involving a well-informed population have to be arrived at, involving those who are concerned about more than just preserving coal- and oil-industry profits and the control of society. Time to wake up to this grand deception and the deceivers behind it, if there is to be any future for this planet.

See:

WeatherWar101: Sofia Smallstorm on Red Ice Radio http://ow.ly/8Fl230bZ1nv

Weather War Big Picture: Geo-Engineering & Bio-Engineering - V.1
http://ow.ly/kd4f30bZ1rl

The Secret of Nikola Tesla http://ow.ly/UFdO30bZ1Os

Endnotes

[1] Pearl Street Station http://ow.ly/gfen30bZ1Un

[2] U.S. Energy Information Administration http://ow.ly/5VuN30bZ1Yo

[3] Air pollution stops rain http://ow.ly/MAKQ30bZ21D

[4] Cloud Condensation Nuclei (CCN) http://ow.ly/LIrM30bZ24q

[5] Stratospheric Welsbach seeding for reduction of global warming US 5003186 A
http://ow.ly/lW2630bZ27A

[6] Radar http://ow.ly/n9dF30bZ2bU

[7] Frequency http://ow.ly/2GJH30bZ2j6

[8] The Myth of HAARP Ring http://ow.ly/FpGZ30bZ2n5

[9] Air Force prepares to dismantle HAARP ahead of summer shutdown

[10] 2014 Multi-function Phased Array Radar software upgrade: Spring release
http://ow.ly/goY630bZ2rs

[11] Cloudbuster – Wilhelm Reich – Orgone Energy

Copyright

WW101 Team

I am always looking for people to join the team, and all genuinely concerned individuals anywhere in the world are invited. As I say frequently, all seven billion of us are in this together, and confronting this really should be the number one priority for us all.

Involvement can range from documenting your local weather, doing time-lapse video, doing research, working on promoting this reality, or any other efforts or resources you can bring to the project. In addition to the rest of this book series, the Big Picture 2.0 movie is the next major endeavor to bring this reality to the people of this planet, and we can use all the help we can get.

If you are interested in standing up for the planet and all life on it, please send an email (weatherwar@gmx.com) with "WW101Team" in the subject, and join the ever-growing group of committed individuals. You will be very glad you did.

WW101

Made in the USA
Middletown, DE
05 January 2020